COELOPHYSIS

A Buddy Book
by
Richard M. Gaines

ABDO
Publishing Company

VISIT US AT
www.abdopub.com

Published by ABDO Publishing Company, 4940 Viking Drive, Edina, Minnesota 55435. Copyright © 2001 by Abdo Consulting Group, Inc. International copyrights reserved in all countries. No part of this book may be reproduced in any form without written permission from the publisher.

Printed in the United States.

Edited by: Christy DeVillier
Contributing editors: Mike Goecke, Matt Ray
Graphic Design: Denise Esner, Maria Hosley
Cover Art: ©Doug Henderson from *How Dinosaurs Came to Be* by Patricia Lauber, published by Simon & Schuster, title page.
Interior Photos/Illustrations: page 4: ©Douglas Henderson from *Riddle of the Dinosaur* by John Noble Wilford, published by Knopf; page 5: Denise Esner; page 7: Joe Tucciarone; pages 8, 19 & 20: ©Douglas Henderson from *Dinosaur Tree* by Douglas Henderson, published by Bradbury Press; page 11: ©Douglas Henderson from *Dinosaurs, A global View* by S&S Czerkas, published by Dragon's World; page 13: Corbis; page 15: Maria Hosley; pages 16 & 25: ©Douglas Henderson from *How Dinosaurs Came to Be* by Patricia Lauber, published by Simon & Schuster; page 17: Douglas Henderson from *Dawn of the Dinosaurs* by Robert A. Lang and Rose Houk, published by the ©Petrified Forest Museum Association; pages 18, 21 & 27: ©Douglas Henderson from *Dinosaur Ghosts* by J. Lynett Gillette, published by Dial; page 23: Jodi Henderson.

Library of Congress Cataloging-in-Publication Data

Gaines, Richard, 1942-
    Coelophysis/Richard M. Gaines.
    p. cm. – (Dinosaurs)
    Includes index.
    ISBN 1-57765-488-9
    1. Coelophysis—Juvenile literature. [1. Coelophysis. 2. Dinosaurs.] I. Title.

QE862.S3 G35 2001
567.912—dc21

                                                           00-069986

TABLE OF CONTENTS

WHAT WERE THEY?

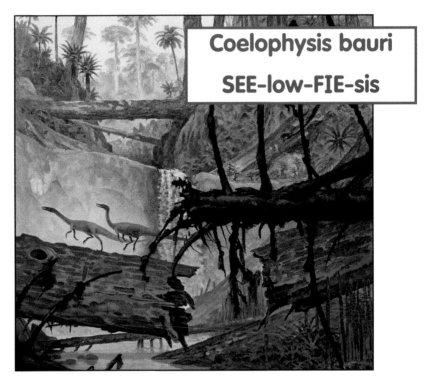

Coelophysis bauri

SEE-low-FIE-sis

Coelophysis bauri was one of the first dinosaurs. This meat-eating, or carnivorous, dinosaur lived during the late Triassic period. That was about 225 million years ago.

The Coelophysis was about nine feet (three m) long. It had large eyes and good eyesight. It had a long tail, a long neck, and a long head. The Coelophysis's hands had three fingers and long claws.

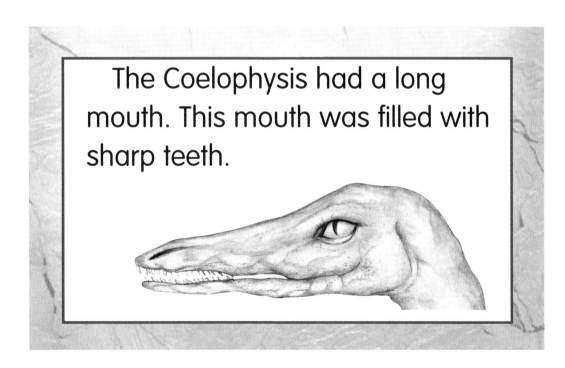

The Coelophysis had a long mouth. This mouth was filled with sharp teeth.

The Coelophysis was quick. It could run as fast as 25 miles (40 km) per hour. This quick dinosaur ran on its two back legs. These back legs were long and straight. So, the Coelophysis could take extra big steps.

Like all dinosaurs, the Coelophysis's legs were underneath its body. This is not true for all reptiles. Other reptiles have legs that stick out from the sides of their bodies. So, their bodies were very close to the ground. It took more energy for these reptiles to run.

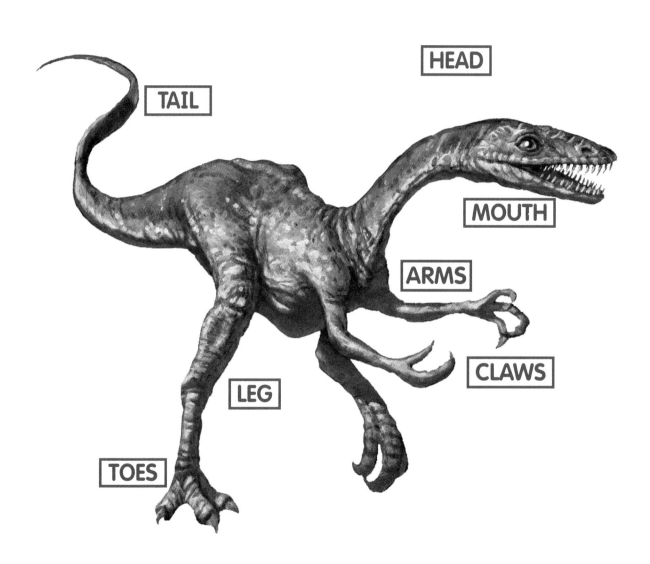

TAIL

HEAD

MOUTH

ARMS

CLAWS

LEG

TOES

The Coelophysis had a long neck.

The Coelophysis had a long neck. It could carry its head high above the ground. The Coelophysis could see very well with its head high above the ground.

There was one problem with the Coelophysis's long neck. This long neck needed blood just like the rest of the body. It was hard for this dinosaur's heart to pump blood upwards into the Coelophysis's long neck.

WHERE DID THEY LIVE?

The Coelophysis lived on the North American continent 225 million years ago. Part of North America was a tropical forest back then.

Many of the trees in these tropical forests were saved as fossils. We call this fossil-filled piece of land the Petrified Forest.

There were volcanoes and mountains south of the Petrified Forest. These volcanoes often blew up and sent ash over the land. This ash helped to save many old animals and trees as fossils.

Volcanoes

LAND OF THE COELOPHYSIS

The Coelophysis lived in a warm rain forest. This forest was full of evergreen, or conifer, trees.

Back then, many streams flowed from the mountains and volcanoes. These streams sometimes flooded the land. This turned the land into a wetland.

Many kinds of plants grew in these wetlands. Some of these plants were cycads and ferns.

Cycads look like large pineapples. Cycad plants can grow about four feet (one m) tall.

Cycad plant

13

THEIR DINOSAUR NEIGHBORS

Dinosaurs were new to North America 225 million years ago. So, the Coelophysis did not have a lot of dinosaur neighbors.

The Anchisaurus is one of the earliest plant-eating dinosaurs. The Anchisaurus belonged to a family of long-necked dinosaurs. This dinosaur is related to the Apatosaurus. The Anchisaurus had a long neck and tail like the Apatosaurus.

The Anchisaurus had teeth shaped like spoons. It used these teeth to rip its food.

This plant-eater swallowed stones from the ground as it ate. We call these rocks gastroliths or gizzard stones. These rocks helped to break down the food in the Anchisaurus's stomach.

Anchisaurus

There were many animals that lived in the water. One of these animals is the Metoposaur. It weighed 1,000 pounds (454 kg) and was 10 feet (3 m) long. It had a big, flat head and sharp teeth.

Metoposaur

Lissodus

Two kinds of fresh water sharks lived there, too. One of these sharks is the Lissodus. It was about six inches (15 cm) long. The Lissodus had flat teeth for eating clams. The Xenacanthus was another shark. This shark was three feet (one m) long.

WHAT DID THEY EAT?

A pack of Coelophysis.

The Coelophysis probably ate any animal it could catch. One of the animals it hunted was the Technosaurus.

The Technosaurus was five feet (two m) long. It weighed about 70 pounds (32 kg). This plant-eating dinosaur had a beak-shaped bone instead of front teeth.

One Coelophysis could catch a Technosaurus. A pack of 10 Coelophysis could kill a 2,000 pound (907 kg) animal like the Placerias.

Placerias

One of the Coelophysis's enemies is the Postosuchus. The Postosuchus was about 12-15 feet (4-5 m) long. It looked like the Tyrannosaurus rex. This meat-eating dinosaur attacked with its large, curved claws.

Postosuchus

The Rutiodon was another enemy of the Coelophysis. It looked like a crocodile of today. The Rutiodon was 20-30 feet (6-9 m) long. This meat-eater lived in the water. The Rutiodon could hide underneath water. Then, it could surprise and attack the Coelophysis when it came near to drink water.

Rutiodon

FAMILY LIFE

Coelophysis mothers watched over their eggs and young carefully. They tried to keep their eggs and young safe from other animals. Coelophysis eggs and young were in danger around other Coelophysis, too.

Older Coelophysis would eat anything they could find. They would even eat young Coelophysis. We call eating your own kind cannibalism. Some of today's crocodiles are cannibals.

Eggs

DISCOVERY

David Baldwin was the first man to discover Coelophysis fossils.

In February, 1881, Baldwin found some thin fossil bones near Chama, New Mexico. He sent them to Professor Edward Drinker Cope.

Cope realized that these fossil bones belonged to a dinosaur nobody knew about. He named the new dinosaur Coelophysis.

In 1895, the American Museum of Natural History in New York bought Cope's Coelophysis fossils.

Coelophysis

DINOSAUR GRAVEYARD

In 1947, Edwin Colbert and his friends found over 200 Coelophysis fossils. They found these fossils in northern New Mexico.

How did these Coelophysis bones turn into fossils? Soon after the Coelophysis died, there was a flood.

The flood carried their bodies to the bottom of a river. Sand and mud covered these dinosaur bodies. Over millions of years, the bodies turned into stone. These stones are what we call fossils.

A pack of Coelophysis in a rain storm.

Paleontologists have studied these fossils. They learned a lot about the Coelophysis. In fact, we know more about the Coelophysis than most other dinosaurs.

American Museum of Natural History
Central Park West at 79th Street
New York, NY 10024
www.amnh.org

Carnegie Museum of Natural History
4400 Forbes Avenue
Pittsburgh, PA 15213
www.clpgh.org/cmnh

Museum of Comparative Zoology
Harvard University
26 Oxford St
Cambridge, MA 02138
www.mcz.harvard.edu

Ruth Hall Paleontology Museum
Ghost Ranch Conference Center
US 84 HC 77 Box 11
Abiquiu, NM 87510-9601

COELOPHYSIS

NAME MEANS	Hollow Bone
DIET	Meat
WEIGHT	50 pounds (23 kg)
LENGTH	3-10 feet (1-3 m)
TIME	Triassic Period
FAMILY	Theropods
SPECIAL FEATURE	Long neck
FOSSILS FOUND	USA–Connecticut, New Mexico

Coelophysis lived 225 million years ago

First humans appeared 1.6 million years ago

Triassic Period	Jurassic Period	Cretaceous Period	Tertiary Period
245 Million years ago	208 Million years ago	144 Million years ago	65 Million years ago
Mesozic Era			Cenozoic Era

29

FUN DINOSAUR WEB SITES

Zoom Dinosaurs
www.EnchantedLearning.com/subjects/dinosaurs
Zoom Dinosaurs, designed for students of all ages, includes an illustrated dinosaur dictionary and classroom activities.

Dino Detectives
www.kids.discovery.com/dinos/dinos.html
Featuring the Coelophysis and other popular dinosaurs, this site is balanced with dinosaur facts and fun stuff including prehistoric postcards, a dino-scope, and contests.

Dinosaur Discovery Room
www.clpgh.org/cmnh/discovery
Presented by the Carnegie Museum of Natural History, this site invites children to learn about dinosaurs through detective games, riddles, and dinosaur jumbles.

IMPORTANT WORDS

cannibalism eating your own kind.

carnivorous meat-eating.

conifer trees that have needles instead of leaves. Conifers stay green all year long.

continent one of the seven large land masses on earth.

cycads palmlike plants or trees.

dinosaur reptiles that lived on the land 248-65 million years ago.

fossil remains of very old animals and plants. People commonly find fossils in the ground.

gastrolith rocks the Anchisaurus ate, or gizzard stones.

paleontologist a scientist who studies very old life (like dinosaurs), mostly by studying fossils.

rain forest a tropical woodland with a lot of rain.

reptile an animal that breathes air, has scales, and lays eggs.

Triassic period period of time that happened 245-208 million years ago.

tropical hot or warm climate.

wetlands land mostly covered with water.

INDEX